HURRICANES!

New and Updated

GAIL GIBBONS

Holiday House · New York

To "Hurricane" Donna

Special thanks to Eric Evenson of the National Weather Service, South Burlington, Vermont; and to Chris Vaccaro of the National Oceanic and Atmospheric Administration.

Copyright © 2009, 2019 by Gail Gibbons
All Rights Reserved
HOLIDAY HOUSE is registered in the U.S.
Patent and Trademark Office.
Printed and Bound in December 2019 at Tien Wah Press,
Johor Bahru, Johor, Malaysia.
Second Edition
www.holidayhouse.com

3 5 7 9 10 8 6 4 2

The Library of Congress has catalogued the prior edition as follows:
Gibbons, Gail.
Hurricanes! / by Gail Gibbons. — 1st ed.
p. cm.
ISBN 978-0-8234-2233-3 (hardcover)
1. Hurricanes—Juvenile literature. I. Title.
QC944.2.G53 2009
551.55'2—dc22
2009008761
ISBN 978-0-8234-4157-0 (hardcover)
ISBN 978-0-8234-4179-2 (paperback)

HURRICANE comes from Hurakan, the name for the Mayan god of storms.

The winds are howling, the rain is pouring down, violent waves are crashing onto the shore. A dangerous spinning storm has formed over tropical waters. It is a hurricane making landfall.

CUMULONIMBUS CLOUDS

EVAPORATES means that water turns into moist air.

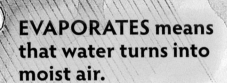

F = Fahrenheit
C = Celsius

All hurricanes form over tropical waters. Warm water evaporates and rises into the atmosphere. The warm moist air spins upward, creating a draft that sucks up more moisture. If the water temperature is more than 80°F (26.6°C), the cycle continues. Winds get stronger. As the moist air rises, very tall cumulonimbus (KYOOM-you-low-NIM-bus) clouds are formed.

mph = miles per hour
kph = kilometers per hour

CONDENSATION occurs when the moist, warm air cools and turns into rain.

The rising air creates even more of an updraft. Even more moisture rises, creating even larger cumulonimbus clouds that hold even more water. The spinning of the air accelerates. Even larger groups of cumulonimbus clouds continue to build up. Condensation causes rain. When the speed of the wind reaches 74 mph (119.1 kph), the storm is classified as a hurricane.

EYE

EYEWALL

EYEWALL

Most hurricanes are about 100 miles (160.9 kilometers) to 300 miles (482.8 kilometers) wide. The center of a hurricane is called the eye, which is clear and calm. It may be 10 to 20 miles (16.1 to 32.2 kilometers) wide. The strongest winds in a hurricane usually surround the eye of the storm, in an area called the eyewall.

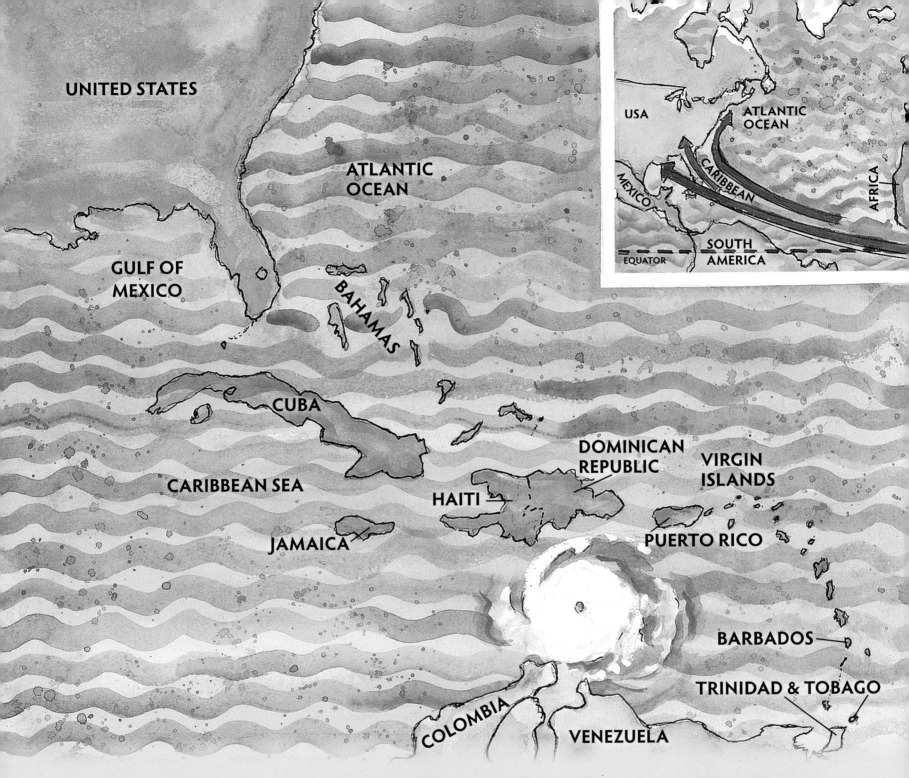

Most hurricanes form over the Atlantic Ocean north of the equator. They usually last about a week and often travel on a westward course.

Many hurricanes have devastated cities and towns with strong winds. Usually there are heavy rains and flooding. Storm surges are huge walls of water forced up out of the sea, devastating everything in their path and on occasion altering the shoreline itself.

The NATIONAL HURRICANE CENTER is located in Miami, Florida.

METEOROLOGISTS are scientists who study weather.

In 1972, Herbert Saffir and Robert Simpson developed the Saffir-Simpson Hurricane Wind Scale. This scale ranks hurricanes in categories of 1 to 5. Satellites, observations, and computer models help meteorologists at the National Hurricane Center predict the likely impact of an approaching hurricane.

CATEGORY 1 HURRICANES

Category 1 hurricanes have wind speeds between 74 mph (119 kph) and 95 mph (153 kph).

There is some damage to trees and small buildings.

CATEGORY 2 HURRICANES

Category 2 hurricanes have wind speeds between 96 mph (154 kph) and 110 mph (177 kph).

Coastal roads flood and there is moderate damage.

13

CATEGORY 3 HURRICANES

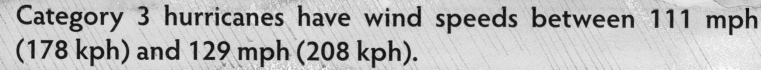

Category 3 hurricanes have wind speeds between 111 mph (178 kph) and 129 mph (208 kph).

Trees are uprooted. Large cars and trucks are swept away. There is extensive damage to buildings and boats.

CATEGORY 4 HURRICANES

Category 4 hurricanes have wind speeds between 130 mph (209 kpm) and 156 mph (251 kpm).

The destruction is devastating. Buildings suffer extreme damage. Roads and bridges are washed away. Boats are tossed about like toys.

CATEGORY 5 HURRICANES

Category 5 hurricanes have winds greater than 157 mph (252 kph). Winds have been recorded at more than 200 mph (321.87 kph).

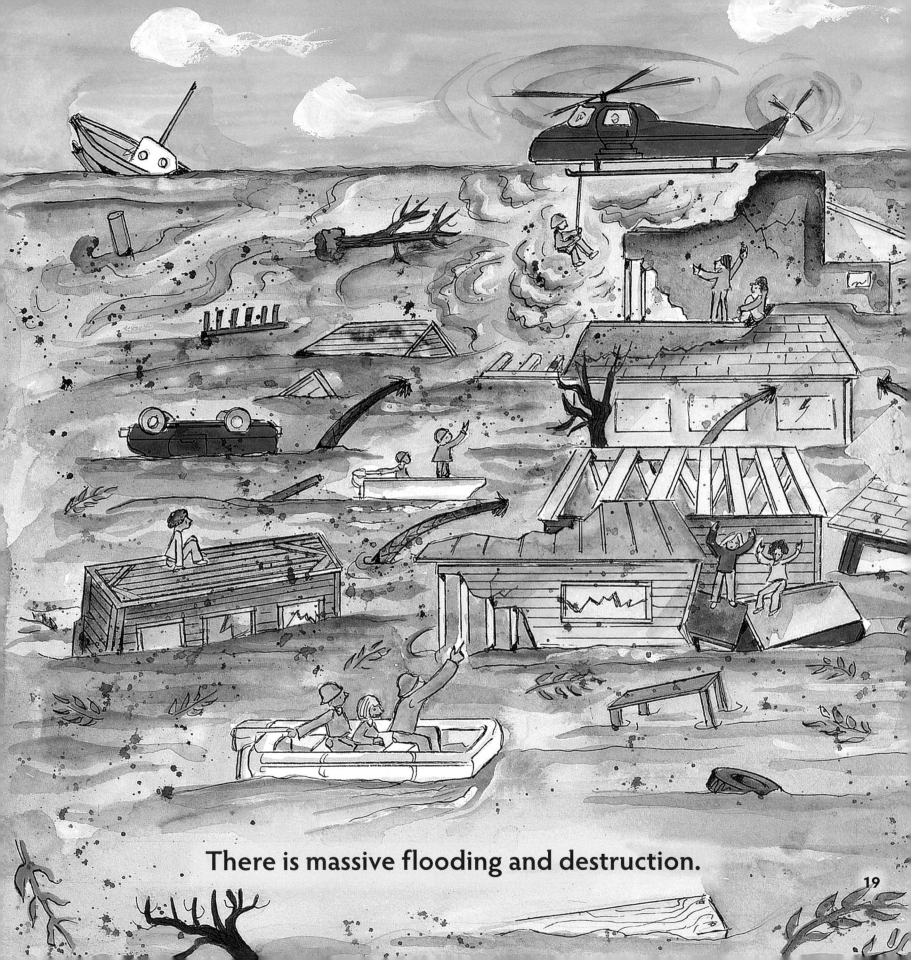

There is massive flooding and destruction.

HURRICANES COME ASHORE . . .

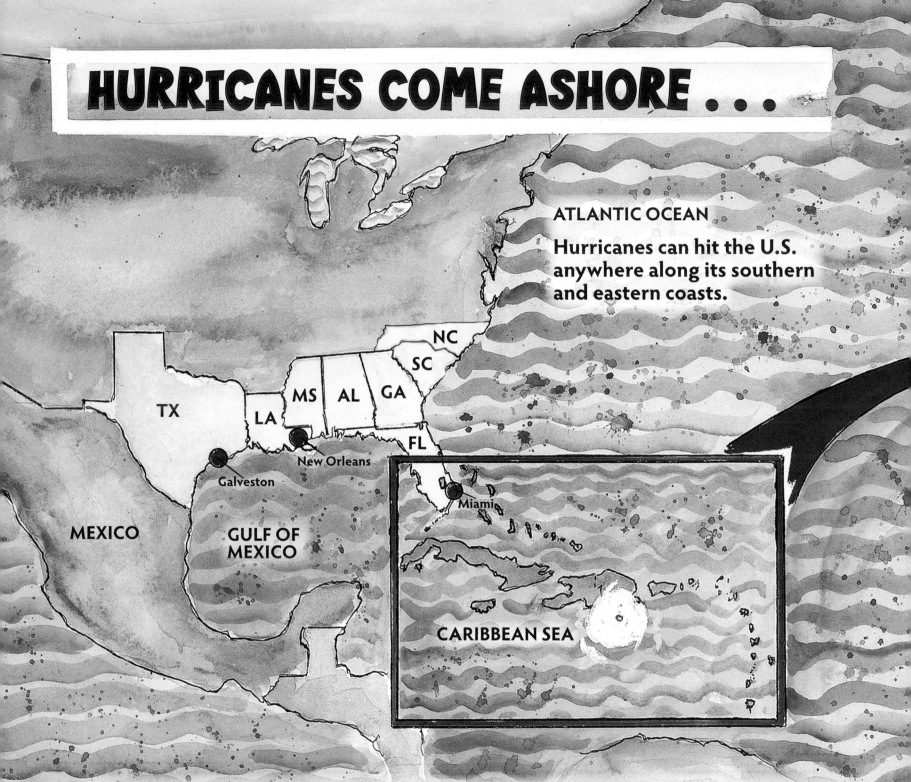

ATLANTIC OCEAN

Hurricanes can hit the U.S. anywhere along its southern and eastern coasts.

NC

SC

TX

LA

MS   AL   GA

FL

New Orleans

Galveston

MEXICO

GULF OF MEXICO

Miami

CARIBBEAN SEA

Most hurricanes do their damage in the Caribbean and along the Gulf Coast and the southeast coast of the United States.

SOUTH AMERICA

EQUATOR

ATLANTIC OCEAN

FL

Miami

BAHAMAS

CUBA

DOMINICAN REPUBLIC

JAMAICA

HAITI

PUERTO RICO

VIRGIN ISLANDS

CARIBBEAN SEA

Most hurricanes are Category 1 or 2. Category 5 hurricanes are rare and have reached land on an average of once every five years.

SOME HURRICANES THROUGHOUT HISTORY

GALVESTON, September 8, 1900

TEXAS

Galveston

GULF OF MEXICO

EXICO

In 1900 the biggest city in Texas was Galveston. On September 8, a huge hurricane struck. The storm surge was 20 feet (6.1 meters) high. It totally destroyed the city, killing about 12,000 people. Scientists later classified it as a Category 5 hurricane.

HURRICANE ANDREW, August 24, 1992

ATLANTIC
OCEAN

GULF OF
MEXICO

FL

Miami

After crossing the Bahamas, Hurricane Andrew hit Florida south of Miami with winds up to 195 mph (313.8 kph). At that time it was the costliest hurricane in U.S. history. Most of the damage was done by the fierce winds. Originally classified as a Category 4 hurricane, it was reclassified as a Category 5.

HURRICANE KATRINA, August 2005

UNITED STATES

MS
LA
AL
ATLANTIC OCEAN
New Orleans
FL
Miami
GULF OF MEXICO

The most damaging hurricane in U.S. history was Hurricane Katrina. It started in the Bahamas, then crossed southern Florida as a Category 1 hurricane. On August 29, it made its final landfall northeast of New Orleans as a powerful Category 3 hurricane.

EVACUATE means to leave and seek safety in another place.

EVACUATION ROUTE

Storm surges resulted in the flooding of 80 percent of New Orleans. More than one million people had to evacuate, and 1,200 people lost their lives. Catastrophic damage was done all along the coastlines of Louisiana, Mississippi, and Alabama.

FORECASTING AND TRACKING HURRICANES

WEATHER SATELLITE

Meteorologists gather information about hurricanes from many sources. Satellites measure the size of a hurricane and can help tell how fast and in what direction a hurricane is moving.

An airplane passes through one side of a hurricane, then through the eye and out the other side.

Hurricane Hunters are members of the Air Force Reserve.

U.S. AIR FORCE

Airplanes are flown into hurricanes by pilots known as Hurricane Hunters. Special instruments dropped by planes measure wind speed, temperature, air pressure, and the amount of moisture in the clouds.

All of the storm's details are gathered and fed into computers. This helps scientists make a new computer model that predicts the size and strength of the storm and what land may be in its path.

A HURRICANE WATCH is a notice that tells people in a certain area that a hurricane might hit within 48 hours.

One flag means **STORM WARNING.**

A HURRICANE WARNING is a notice telling people that a hurricane is likely to hit within 36 hours.

Two flags mean **HURRICANE WARNING.**

These predictions help determine if an area will need to be evacuated. When necessary, the National Hurricane Center will issue hurricane watches and warnings that are made public on radio, television, the Internet, and mobile devices. The U.S. Coast Guard raises flags.

Many hurricanes may be forming at one time. Giving them names makes it easier to track them.

In 1953 weather officials started naming hurricanes after women, with the first storm of the season being given a woman's name beginning with the letter *A*, the second storm a name beginning with the letter *B*, and so on. In 1979 men's names started to be used as well. The names of some of the worst storms have been retired and will not be used again. Andrew and Katrina are two of these.

WHEN A HURRICANE IS APPROACHING . . .

There should be a plan to evacuate. Everyone should know the route.

Cover the windows of your house with plywood to prevent flying glass.

Have a battery-powered radio on hand to hear all alerts.

Turn off the electricity to your house before you evacuate.

Select a person outside the hurricane area who can inform other family members of your status.

Take care of your family pets.

Pick up loose items in your yard and put them away. They can become dangerous in strong winds.

HAVE AN ADULT HELP YOU.

Make sure the family supply kit is ready.

✓ WATER
✓ NONPERISHABLE FOODS
✓ FLASHLIGHT
✓ FRESH BATTERIES
✓ FIRST-AID KIT
✓ BATTERY-POWERED RADIO
✓ RAINWEAR

MORE INTERESTING FACTS...

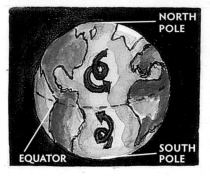

Hurricanes north of the equator rotate counterclockwise. Hurricanes south of the equator rotate clockwise.

The deadliest storm on record is a cyclone in Bangladesh in 1970. More than 300,000 people died.

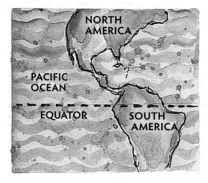

Cyclones are hurricane-like storms that form over the western Pacific Ocean.

The evaporation of about two billion tons (1.8 billion metric tons) of water a day can occur while a hurricane is building up over the ocean.

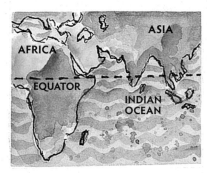

Typhoons are hurricane-like storms that form over the Indian Ocean.

WEBSITES

In the United States:
http://www.hurricanes.gov

Visit www.Ready.gov for safety information from the Federal Emergency Management Agency (FEMA).

In Canada:
http://www.Canada.ca/en /environment-climate-change /services/hurricane-forecast-facts.html

Signs mark evacuation routes.